Network Marketing Selling Secrets

50 Ways to Get New Customers

By Argena Olivis

www.networkmarketingkingdom.com

Bonus Video: How to Get Leads and Customers Online

Subscribe to Get Free Tips On How To Generate Leads and Get Customers

When you subscribe to get network marketing tips via email, you will get free access to exclusive subscriber-only resources. All you have to do is enter your email address to the right to get instant access.

These resources will help you get more out of your business – to be able to reach your goals, have more motivation, be at your best, and live the life you've always dreamed of. I'm always adding new resources, which you will be notified of as a subscriber. These will help you get an endless amount of leads and customers.

**Visit
www.networkmarketingkingdom.com/video
to Access The Bonus Video**

Introduction

I want to thank and congratulate you for reading the book, *"Network Marketing Selling Secrets: 50 Ways to Get New Customers."*

This book contains 50 proven ways to get customers in your network marketing company.

If you're looking for fresh ideas on how to increase your sales this week, look no further.

You will find some unique ways to increase your customer base, as well as some ways you may have heard of before, but never took action on.

Discover how getting customers both online and offline will increase you and your team's chances for success.

Many networkers are using the same strategies. You want to plant seeds in many different ways so you'll always have a stream of new customers coming in.

Learn how to master one way of getting customers, and move on to master another. Once you find out what's working best, use and improve that strategy to make it even better.

If you take action on these selling secrets, you will already be ahead of most - because most people don't take action.

Don't you think it's time you start putting in the work necessary to live the lifestyle you want?

We all want more time with the family and the freedom to do what we want whenever we want without money being an object.

You cannot make money without others, so it's best to try to help as many people as you can, and always add value so people will be willing to pay you.

Your goal should be to become the "go-to" person for your product, to win customers over, so they are loyal to you, and recommend you to their friends and family.

If you're not making money or getting any customers, it may be because you're not adding enough value. But through these selling strategies, I'll show you how to do so.

I'm sure you got into network marketing because you wanted something better.

Well, in this book is an opportunity to create more freedom in your life by making more money in your business.

Thanks again for reading Network Marketing Selling Secrets, I hope you enjoy it!

Table of Contents

Chapter 1: Ways to Get Customers Offline

First, we are going to go into ways to get customers offline. Getting customers offline can be known as active marketing.

This means you are actively engaging with people and meeting people.

Active marketing is the fastest way to get new customers when trying to get customers online; it takes time to build a trusting relationship.

A lot of people miss the one-on-one communication with those they are buying from.

Therefore, your chances of getting customers offline are very high.

This book is intended to help you find new customers. But remember: it's harder to find new customers than get returning customers.

So, after you've found some new customers, make sure to have outstanding customer service. They'll always return back to you and only you.

Way #1: Vendor Shows

Vendor shows are events put on by organizations or other small business owners like yourself.

I'm big on vendor shows because I got a lot of leads this way.

To get customers at vendor shows, you don't necessarily need to have product on hand-- but that is ideal.

When a potential customer approaches your table, make sure to be very welcoming.

Have a form ready for them to fill out where they can be entered into a giveaway. You always want to collect contact information, no matter what.

Offer them something. Give them a sample.

If you have products on hand to sell, be knowledgeable about them, and answer all their questions.

If they end up buying something from you, make sure to put your sales material or business card in their shopping bag.

Also, make sure to collect their contact information by having them fill out a raffle ticket or document.

Keep notes about new customer names and what they purchased from you. Then follow up with them in a few days and ask how they're enjoying whatever they purchased.

If they don't purchase anything, still make it your business to meet them and get to know them a little better.

So, if they take a sample, you can follow up with them later to ask if they enjoyed the sample.

Way #2: Flea Markets

Flea markets are similar to vendor shows. Find flea markets in your area by searching through Google.

The best way to win at a flea market is to be a constant presence. Customers may get used to seeing you there and recommend you to their friends.

Also, keep in mind that many people go to flea markets to get discounted items.

You may want to entice a lead by offering them lower priced items, items that others have returned, or a discount you've made up yourself.

Way #3: Sales Material Drop

This is when you leave your sales material or promotional material for your company in high traffic areas or places you know people are waiting to get service.

Many companies have some type of books or pamphlets that they give out, or that the consultants have to buy, that lets customers know more about the product or to showcase the products they offer.

If your company doesn't offer this, create your own documents.

What I mean by drop is to "leave." So, leave your sales material in places, such as doctors' offices, local businesses, and any other places that people are waiting to get serviced.

Way #4: Hanging Sales Materials On Doorknobs

Hanging your promotional materials on doorknobs is a great way to increase your customer base.

Simply put your sales material in clear bags that will fit nicely and look professional on a door knob and leave them at houses in your neighborhood.

Do this a few times around your neighborhood until you start getting results. Then move on and expand your reach into different areas.

Way #5: Business Appreciation

Call businesses that have employees that may be interested in what product you sell.

Tell them that they were nominated your business of the week. Ask if you can stop by and give everyone in the office free samples.

When you go to drop off the samples, make sure to have your sales material with you. This will also be a good time to do a raffle.

Have the people in the office fill out the raffle forms; you can come back for the forms at a later date. Now you have successfully collected names, emails, and possibly phone numbers.

Make sure to follow up with all the people who have entered into your raffle to see if they liked the samples.

Way #6: Meet Ups

Find groups in your city that you are interested in. It doesn't matter what type of group it is. Make some friends and simply tell them what you do.

They may be interested or know someone who is interested in your products.

You can go to www.meetup.com to find these groups.

Way #7: Garage sales

Host a garage sale or find out if someone in your family or friends will be having one anytime soon.

Make sure to put out your sales materials, samples, and products you have on hand.

Many people love garage sales and it'll be another way to get your name out there.

Way #8: Local Chamber of Commerce

Sign up for your local chamber of commerce.

They will let you know when there are meetings in your area and you'll get the heads-up on events that are happening in your neighborhood.

Way #9: Parties

Host a party or have someone else host a party.

You can have it at your place or rent out an area. Either way, make it happen.

If you see that you're getting customers this way, start hosting more parties.

Way #10: Employee Appreciation

Contact businesses and ask them if you can set up an employee appreciation for them.

Do something nice for the employees that work for their company. For example: If you sell weight loss products, then give each employee a free consultation.

Way #11: Set Up Outside or Inside of Businesses

Ask local businesses if you can do a customer appreciation for them. When you set up your table, give out something to the people approaching or leaving the store.

When contacting business owners, let them know what's in it for them. Tell them you'll be giving out free items to customers or that you'll give discounts to the customers who buy something from their business.

Also, tell them to keep in mind that you'll be trying to get customers in the door.

Way #12: Advertising

Depending on your budget you can start advertising. Consider doing a billboard or putting up a yard sign in your yard.

Any exposure is great. Make sure to always leave business

cards or fliers in local businesses that allow it.

Way #13: Sample Packs

Sample packs are packs that you create using samples and other goodies. Buy professional looking plastic bags from the dollar store and put samples, a business card, a fund-raising flier, and candy in them.

Hand them out to people while doing errands or when you're just out and about.

Way #14: Business Cards In Books

Go to the library and look for the book section that is relevant to the product you're trying to sell. Put your business cards in all the books.

You can also do the same thing in bookstores.

If you do this method, make sure to have your company website on your cards.

I remember someone actually contacted me after finding my business card in a book. It was like six months after the fact.

Way #15: Business Cards at ATM

Leave your business cards at the ATM. Also, leave it at gas

stations.

Way #16: Consultations

Offer free consultations to people that may be able to benefit from your product.

Way #17: Post Cards

Send out postcards to people in your area letting them know that you are the one representing your company in that area.

There are services that tell you all the addresses in the neighborhood and will also send out the card for you.

Way #18: Canvassing

Go door-to-door and let people know what you do and what you have to offer.

Be careful; make sure not to do this alone.

Way #19: Fundraising

Set up fundraisers with customers.

Seek out groups that can benefit from doing fundraisers, such as school groups and clubs in your area.

Way #20: Raffles

Sell raffle tickets and auction off your products at different events.

Or do raffles with existing customers. Tell your customers that for every customer they refer to you, they'll get another raffle ticket for free to put in the pot.

Way #21: Coupons

Create coupons and give them out to potential customers.

Also, offer your own sales on your products.

Offer a discount to first-time customers.

Way #22: Open House

Host an open house. An open house will require you to have products on hand.

Allow people to come in and view what products you have to offer, and buy them.

Also, let them know of upcoming products so they can pre-order.

You can do this at your place with your warm market, which is your family, friends, and associates. Or you can do it at a local place in the community and allow the general public to attend.

Make sure to advertise this well; it's more likely for people to show up for a party than an open house.

Be sure to give out samples and sample packs.

Way #23: Phone Calls To Warm Market

Make phone calls to your warm market.

Let them know you're in business. Chances are they'll buy from you or help you to get customers.

Way #24: Referrals

The best way to get referrals is to have outstanding customer service. Make your customer service so outstanding that people can't wait to share the experience with others.

As I've mentioned before, it's easier to get an existing customer to order from you again than to get a new one.

Create a loyal customer base by returning calls and emails in a timely manner, saying thank you every time, following up with them, knowing what they like, etc.

Way #25: Advertising

Advertise your company. Always wear your company logo, use car signs, name tags, bags/purses, etc.

Chapter 2: Ways to Get Customers Online

In order to get customers online, you may have to learn some internet marketing. If you master a few of these ways, it's possible that you can go online completely and make money from home.

To get customers online, you have to be super disciplined and consistent. You can do it, but it will take time.

If you don't have a lot of time, you can outsource a lot of these tasks. Consider hiring a virtual assistant to do your social media management.

Way #26: Facebook

This is most likely where most of your potential customers are hanging out. It's the biggest social media platform-- almost everyone has a Facebook.

Create a Facebook Business Page/Fan Page and create a Facebook Group.

Share valuable and relevant content on your page. Keep in mind: social media is used for building relationships-- it's not a place to spam your website link everywhere.

Be very strategic about how you will provide value to your fans.

Share things such as:

- images

- quotes

- videos

- blog posts

- events

- lifestyle

- tips

If you offer valuable and likable content on your page, people will buy from you, or buy from you again.

You can create images using different apps on your phone or using services, such as www.picmonkey.com or www.canva.com. The app I use to create quote images on my phone is called Word Swag.

Update your page regularly and be yourself.

Way #27: YouTube

I'm willing to bet most of the people in your company are not doing videos on YouTube.

Some may be, most are not.

This is a great way to stand out to your customers.

Create videos that will help them, such as tutorials, demonstrations, or reviews.

Let them know when sales are going on.

Allow people to connect with you through your videos, create some videos about your lifestyle, or day in the life.

Always remember to market your Facebook Fan Page in your YouTube description. Also, post your new videos to your Facebook pages.

Way #28: Google +

Google + is another way to get customers. Make sure to make use of hashtags.

Hashtags are when you put a "#" sign in front of a keyword that you want to be found for.

Post your YouTube Videos to Google +.

Way #29: Pinterest

Pinterest is a very visual social media platform. Many women use this site.

Pinterest is basically all images, but you can also add YouTube videos.

Get customers by marketing your products, sales, discounts, and promo codes.

Make use of hashtags too.

You can even take pictures of blog posts or other offers your running in order to entice customers to shop at your store.

Way #30: Website

Create a website to promote your business. Make sure you are following your company's terms and conditions.

Your best bet is to create a website around the product you sell.

Provide value by helping people solve problems.

You can use this website to drive traffic to your company site where they can purchase products.

You can also use your website to create another income stream through advertising, product creation, email marketing, and affiliate marketing.

For a step-by-step tutorial on how to create a website, go to http://www.networkmarketingkingdom.com/website/

Way #31: Email Marketing

Use e-mail marketing software like Aweber to collect names and emails online.

By building an e-mail list, you can send your customers emails about offers, and let them know why they should shop with you instead of the other distributors in your company.

Provide your subscribers with valuable content that is relevant.

In turn, your customers will grow to like and trust you.

Visit http://www.argenaolivis.com/email-marketing-101/ for step-by-step instructions on how to get started with e-mail marketing.

Way #32: Yahoo Answers

Yahoo! answers is a hidden jewel and many marketers haven't tapped into this strategy yet.

Look for people asking questions related to the products you sell. Offer them help.

Leave thorough answers to questions. Personalize the answer by using the person's first name.

Stand out and really provide that person with value. Then leave a link back to your website or your online store.

Make your Yahoo! profile stand out by adding a picture of yourself and links to ways that people can get in touch with you.

There's also a section on your profile that allows you to fill out personal questions about yourself; answer them.

If you decide to make this one of your strategies, answer questions daily. You can be ranked higher if people vote your question as the best answer.

You get points for just signing in to answer questions too.

Way #33: Instagram

Instagram is a social media platform that can bring you a lot of business if used the right way.

To be successful on Instagram, make use of hashtags (like on Google Plus). Instagram requires the use of their app to post pictures. So make sure to download the app on your phone.

Facebook actually owns Instagram, and it's really becoming very popular for marketers, especially the younger generation.

Post pictures and very short videos on Instagram to engage your audience.

If you put hashtags under your images and videos, you are more likely to be found. When people enjoy what you're posting, they have the opportunity to follow you.

When posting hashtags, don't put them directly in the post; put them in a comment beneath your post. This allows you to delete and add tags at a later time without having to take down the entire post.

Another trick is to use your location settings as a call to action. For example, in the location settings, you can put "click the link in bio."

The things that work best on Instagram are:

- inspirational quote images

- personal lifestyle images

- quick videos that give out tips

You can also use Instagram to market your blog and products.

You are only allowed one "clickable link" and that's in your author bio. My suggestion would be to put your store link up.

Way #34: Guest Posting

Guest post on blogs. Guest posting is when you write an article for a popular blog in your niche.

It will be on someone else's blog, but if that blogger is getting traffic, you may be able to grow your own audience, and in turn, get more customers.

After the blog or before the blog, the blogger allows you to add information about yourself and where people can find you at online. Sometimes they'll even allow you to put a link to your squeeze page or landing page so you can grow your e-mail list.

This is a great opportunity to send more traffic to your website or store.

The first step is to find a popular blog that is related to the products you sell. Then e-mail the blogger and ask if you can do a guest blog on their site.

Make sure your blog post is super high quality so people will want to connect with you.

Way #35: Squidoo

Squidoo.com is a place where you can post articles on a blogging platform that's already getting traffic.

Use the right keywords and make sure the article you write is relevant to the product you sell.

You are allowed to put links back to your website or store.

Just like guest posting, if the article is high-quality, people will want to learn more about what you have to offer.

Way #36: SlideShare

SlideShare is a place that you can create a group of slides that inform people on a particular topic of your choosing.

Create a slideshow presentation that tells someone how to do something. Then, make sure to put a link back to your products or website.

Make sure to use relevant keywords in your title and throughout the presentation.

Way #37: Twitter

Twitter is one of the more popular social media platforms; you most likely already have an account.

The great thing about Twitter is that it's a live search engine. So, whatever phrase you search for on Twitter, you can find people talking about that subject in real time.

This is great for getting customers. Do a search for some of the products you have and see if someone is talking about purchasing or looking for a "good one."

For example: If your company sells lipstick, search for "lipstick" in the Twitter search bar, and see if anyone is looking for a recommendation. If they are saying things like "need a new lipstick," then follow them, and start a conversation with them. Do not try to sell to them; just try to help solve their problem. So, in this situation, you may want to say something like, "oh, what kind do you usually get?"

Keep in mind that this is another great place to use hashtags. And to really get noticed, talk about what's trending.

Way #38: Advertise On Websites

This will take a money investment, but can be well worth it. Have the right mindset. Don't think about how much it's going to cost you; think about how much it's going to make you.

Look to advertise on sites that are talking about something relevant to the company you're in.

If the site is getting a lot of visitors, ask the owner how much it costs to advertise on their website.

Sometimes they will already have a page that discusses how much it costs to advertise.

It's just your job to test this strategy out and see how much return you get from it.

Way #39: Forums

Join and participate in forums that are similar to the type of company you are in.

Help people out in the forums, similar to the strategy with Yahoo! Answers.

The more helpful you are to someone, the more likely they are to check out what you have to offer.

Just provide people with information and help people out as much as you can.

What goes around comes around.

Way #40: Directories

Submit your business website to directories online.

People look at directories to find different websites they are looking for.

There are some free ones and some paid ones.

Way #41: Webinars

Host a webinar to get customers. Webinars are like seminars, but online.

Provide them with valuable information that is related to your product and put on a live show to help them with what they're struggling with.

Webinars can be live or recorded.

After you have provided the valuable information, sell your products at the end.

I'm sure there are not many people in your company using this strategy-- this is a great way to get ahead!

Way #42: E-Parties

Host a party online.

You can do this by creating a Facebook event or group.

You can set it up to where if people order from your website between a certain window of time, they get a discount.

There are many ways to do this: create a video, do a live webinar, or just provide them with all the information on Facebook.

You can really host the party anywhere online. Just have a start and end time and give people a reason to want to "come" to the party.

Way #43: Giveaways

Host a giveaway on your YouTube channel.

This is also a way to get more Facebook likes, get people on your email list, or get traffic to your store.

When you do a giveaway, offer a product, or a product bundle, people will really want to enter.

Give the people directions on what they have to do to "enter to win."

The great thing about this is only one person wins, and you still have collected leads.

People may go back to your store and order the product even if they don't win.

Have a start and end date. Tell viewers when you're going to select the winner and do a follow-up video.

Way #44: Contests

Contests are another way to expand your customer base.

You can make the contest relevant to your product line.

For example: If you sell weight-loss products, then you can do a "lose 10 pounds in a month" contest. Whoever wins, give them something cool.

With this, you can either draw a name or give everyone who has won a prize. It doesn't have to be a physical prize. You can give out an eBook or something else digital.

But this is a great way to promote your products and build a community while having fun.

Way #45: Promo Codes/ Sales / Discounts

People love to save money. Always make it known when you offer free shipping or promo codes that can save your customers a few bucks.

These are great because they have an end date, which will inspire the customer to take action right away.

Way #46: eBook

Write an eBook relevant to what you sell.

You can charge for it or make it free for those who opt-in to your email list.

From there you can promote your products if it will help them to solve a particular problem they're struggling with.

Get my free course on how to create a kindle book by visiting: http://www.argenaolivis.com/freekindlecourse

Way #47: PPC

Use a pay-per-click campaign with an advertising company.

The advertising company will show your ads to prospects, and you can have a link straight to your store, to your website, or to your email list.

You can also do a Facebook Ads campaign.

Paid traffic is something to truly consider these days. Although, if you're consistent with getting free traffic, then that's great.

But paid traffic gives you more security. Once you know the numbers, how much it costs to acquire a customer, you're already winning the game.

There are many advertising companies. You don't have to go with any big ones like Google Adwords. But regardless of whatever company you choose, I highly recommend taking a course on it first so you don't waste a ton of money.

Way #48: Testimonials

Use testimonials from people that have used your product and tell people about it through your blog, eBooks, ads, or wherever you market online.

People are more likely to invest in things they see are getting results.

You can also use testimonials from your current customers about your outstanding customer service. This will set you apart from others.

Also, use things such as before and after photos on your social media.

Way #49: Product Demos

Product demonstrations are another way to get customers.

Walk customers through the entire process step-by-step on how to use your products.

You can do this through videos, blog posts, emails, eBooks, etc.

Post product demos to your social media and promote them on your website.

This will show that you know what you're doing, and you will be seen as an expert on whatever you're selling.

Way #50: Referrals/Getting Content Shared

When you share amazing content online, people will begin to notice.

Post things that you yourself would share.

This could be things like inspiring pictures, uplifting messages, or just something funny.

Be shareable online and you begin to see profits come in.

Sometimes it's best to ask for the share. Tell your fans to share a piece of content and give them a reason to.

Chapter 3: Piecing It All Together

In order to get customers, you're going to have to pick only a few ways and see which ways are giving you the biggest return on your investment.

So right now, write down the two ways you will start to get customers.

Although we've gone over 50 ways to get customers, focus is still important, so you can make sure you're being super productive and efficient every day.

It's called the 80/20 rule: 20% of what you do will result in 80% of your customers.

So remember to focus on one company, on two strategies, and see how they work for you.

Then set up a game plan. For example: How many vendor shows do you want to do next week? How often are you willing to post on Facebook? etc.

Create your game plan and set goals for what you plan on doing. Then, starting today-- take action on the strategies and see what results you get.

If you see a strategy not working after three or so weeks, drop it and move on to the next.

Some online strategies may take longer-- but you are planting seeds and many of the things you post, such as videos, will always be up to collect leads for you no matter what you are doing and where you are for years to come.

You never know what a potential customer's situation is; they may come back next week after they get paid and give you a call or shop at your store online.

Give it time; it will require patience, but it also requires consistency.

Be consistent

If you find that a strategy works, do more of it and be consistent with it.

No matter the strategy, you should have a set schedule for when you are going to prospect for customers.

Stick to it, and you're bound to see results.

My recommendation is to focus on only two strategies in a given week. This will let you know how well it's working, and if you should ramp it up or slow it down.

Referrals

Referrals are the best customers because you get them without having to go out and search for them.
Have outstanding customer service and your referral rate will skyrocket!
All in all, you do have what it takes to be successful.
Consistent action will get you the results!

The Takeaway

Work on your mindset. In this business, if you don't believe you can do it, unfortunately, you won't get far.

Invest in yourself. Educate yourself and focus on self-growth.

Never come from a selfish place; always be thinking how you can serve your customers and fans better.

Have an abundance mindset. There's plenty of customers to go around. Mastermind with like-minded people and find a mentor.

Manage your money well and make sure you're turning a profit in your business. Take this seriously and you will succeed!

I'm happy that you got to the end of this book. I have given you 50 proven ways to get customers. What will you do with the information?

Success = Take action, get some results, share the results, repeat.

Conclusion

Thank you again for reading *Network Marketing Selling Secrets*!

I hope this book was able to help you to find strategies that will increase your customer base.

The next step is to use one of these strategies and take consistent action.

Finally, if you enjoyed this book, then I'd like to ask you for a favor. Would you be kind enough to leave a review for this book on Amazon? It'd be greatly appreciated!

Thank you and good luck!

Preview of 'Internet Marketing For Network Marketers"

Chapter 1: Website Creation Strategy

Creating a website is the first thing you'll need to do in order to take your business online. If you truly want to create a business that works 24/7, no matter if you're there or not, you will need a website.

Creating a website is actually quite simple, but it's the upkeep and consistency that will determine your success in the end.

Just like building a company offline, online will take work-- maybe even more work. But that's just in the beginning.

By setting up a website to bring you leads all day, you will be ahead of most people in the industry.

To get even further ahead, you will need to constantly add valuable content to your website. which will, in turn, help build your team or get you more customers.

What Will Your Website Be About?

As a network marketer, your website's subject will depend on what you're trying to do. Would you like to generate leads or customers?

You can always go back and create another website, but for

now, think about what you want to focus on.

The thing about success is you have to focus. What is the one thing that will bring you closer to your goal right now?

Is it having customers so you can have "right now money" and share the results, which, in turn, will help to bring in more recruits?

Or is it bringing in more recruits, which, in turn, will define you as a leader and attract even more recruits?

Creating A Website to Get Customers

Building a website to generate customers will be simple, but you need to know some basic things.

Do not use your company's name on your website. This is for two reasons: 1) it's most likely against your company's guidelines and 2) you want to brand yourself in order to build trust with the leads that come in.

On this website you'll be creating content that has to do with your company's products. For example, if your company sells shoes, you want to create pages that helps people with making shoe selections, finding the right shoe, finding quality shoes, etc.

All your content on your website will be centered around one subject.

This is called a "niche site." A niche site is when you focus on one particular subject and create content around it.

If your content is valuable and helps the customer out, they will want to buy from you. This is when you can send them over to your company website, where they'll make their purchases. More on this later.

Creating A Website to Get Recruits

Creating a site for recruits will be similar to creating a website for customers.

Again, make sure not to mention your company's name. You will be branding yourself.

Branding yourself is when you're using your name and not your company's name while providing value through your website content.

You don't want to mention your company's name because they are already branded. You want leads to join your team because of you.

Anyone can join a company; people will only stick around if they see you as a person that can help them get what they want.

You'll be creating content that helps other network marketers. Think about the problems other network marketers just like you are having and solve them.

Once you do this you will create trust and be looked at as the "go-to" person for network marketing.

In turn, they will either want to join your team or buy any information products and training you may have. More on information product creation later.

There is also an alternative for this if you truly want more targeted leads. You can create a website that is focused on helping people in your particular company.

So, when people search for more information about your company, you will have a site that has all the information they were looking for.

Leads will feel they have an advantage by joining your team because the content you've created for them is valuable and you look like you know what you're doing.

Why You Shouldn't Create a Website For Free

There are many sites out there like blogger.com and wordpress.com that allow you to set up an account and create a website for free.

I'm against these types of sites for many reasons.

The first reason is professionalism. Creating a website that has an URL ending with WordPress or Blogger will look unprofessional.

People will take you and your business more seriously when you use a domain name that ends in .com.

Also, if you go with those free sites you will not own your content. Whoever hosts your site will.

You also won't be able to monetize it the way you want to. Many of those sites have restrictions against things, such as affiliate links and your own ads.

If you're not serious, and you're just dabbling in network marketing, then you can create one of these websites. Just keep in mind that you will be giving up all control.

There are many benefits to using trustworthy hosting

companies. You get customer support and you can create unlimited websites. This means you won't have to buy more hosting in order to create another site.

How to Create a Website

Now we're going to go into how to create an actual website. If you already own a website or blog you can move onto the next section.

Domain Name Rules

A domain name is the web address you type into a browser in order to get to a website. For example: Google.com is a domain name.

There are a few rules you need to follow when naming your website.

- Your domain name should have relevant keywords on what your site will be about

- Avoid using your company name

- Make sure to use .com

- Avoid using dashes

- Should be short and easy to remember

-

Registering A Domain Name

If you buy hosting first, sometimes you'll be able to get a free domain name with the host you choose.

I buy all my domain names from Go Daddy because it allows for all of them to be in one place. You'll learn more about why you may want more than one domain name in later chapters.

Also, if you ever want to switch your hosting for any reason, you will not have to worry about transferring your domain name.

Transferring a domain name from one host to another can take up to three months.

To avoid all of this, just register your domain name with Go Daddy. So, if you ever want to change your host or use the domain name for something else, you can easily just go in and do it.

Register your domain name in Go Daddy by going to www.Godaddy.com and typing in the domain name you came up with of in the search box. Make sure to use the guidelines mentioned above.

If your first possible domain name is taken, think of another one. Keep trying until you find one that sounds right, looks right, and works for you.

Make sure you buy a .com because this is the most universal ending for domain names and you will not encounter any trouble if using this.

Tip: To get the best price on your domain name, search Google for "Go Daddy Promo Codes."

Set Up Hosting

Next you need to decide who you want to host your website. There are many options to go with. There are a ton of hosts you can use.

Find out which is best for you. First, make sure that the host offers a platform that you can easily set up WordPress.

I use a company called Bluehost. To buy hosting with them go to Bluehost.com. I recommend them because they have outstanding customer service and you can easily set up WordPress.

After finding a host, install WordPress, and you're good to go.

For a complete tutorial on how to set up your website visit www.networkmarketingkingdom.com/website

The Website Creation Strategy

Now that you've registered your domain, you've set up WordPress, you're ready to start creating content.

The content you create is what will constantly bring leads into your funnel so you can turn them into customers and recruits.

The goal here is to create content related to your particular product if you're trying to reach customers, or your knowledge of the industry if you're trying to get recruits.

Really find your niche. For example: If your product is related to makeup you can create a website with content about makeup tips, tutorials, product reviews, etc.

Avoid using your company name. Before you create any pages

make sure you use Google Keywords Tool to find keywords to use in your pages that are not too high in competition and now too low.

There are also paid tools that can help with your keyword research and finding keywords that people are searching for. This may be worth it if you want to do in depth research or find keywords and competition.

This will allow your site to rank in Google. Use search engine optimization (SEO) to get found for different words and phrases so you can drive traffic to your site.

My favorite WordPress plugin to use for this is WordPress Yoast SEO. Yoast SEO shows you how to optimize your pages and posts for the search engines.

As you can see, internet marketing is a huge learning curve. There is so much to learn; it is a lot of work.

Your website's keywords are only one way you will get traffic to your website though. You will also get traffic from e-mail and social media marketing. More on that later.

Traffic is very important. There are a tons of ways to get traffic and you want to expose your site to as many people possible.

The equation is simple. More traffic equals more leads.

The thing that will make you successful at creating a website that stands out is you have to create content for a very targeted audience. The content you create has to teach someone how to do something.

When teaching others how to do something, make sure if they follow your blueprint that they'll get results.

After getting results from using your free content, they'll become raving fans, and buy any product or service you have to offer in the future.

Raise your standards when it comes to creating your content. Do the research that is necessary and don't be lazy about it.

If you truly put your all into your website, you will stick out from all the other marketers trying to do the exact same thing. In turn, people will become attracted to you because you will be known as an expert in whatever you're teaching.

The websites that do best are the ones that teach someone how to do something.

Keep in mind that you can easily create more than one website. If you use a host that allows you to have unlimited domains, you can create lots of websites and only pay for hosting once a year. To create a new site all you'd have to do is buy a new domain name.

So you'll be able to create sites for recruiting, getting customers, and possibly one for your team.

As long as you are creating lots of content that is valuable and use the proper keywords, you will generate traffic.

You may be wondering why I don't suggest you create a blog. This is because a blog will constantly have to be updated.

You want a static website that allows you to create something once and leave everything else up to the automated system.

So make sure the content you create is evergreen and not about events or subjects that are time dependent. If you create content that is not evergreen you can use it in your social media updates.

Creating a Team Site

Creating a team site is the best way to leverage your time. If you put out valuable content on another website or through other channels, such as social media or e-mail, then people will want to join your team.

People will also want to join your team once they see the professionalism you have by having a dedicated team site. The best way to get more team members is to get results and share results. In turn, this will attract others and they'll want to do what you're doing.

Make your team site a membership site exclusive only to your team members. Here, you can walk them step-by-step through the process after they sign up to join your team.

You can also offer them training and everything they need to be successful on your team.

This will allow you to leverage your time. You will not have to answer the same questions over and over again. If you put everything you would say to a new team member on that site, you will save them and you time.

There are many ways to get a lead's contact information both online and offline without being invasive......

Visit www.NetworkMarketingKingdom.com to Check Out the Rest of **Internet Marketing For Network Marketers**

Check Out My Other Books

Below you'll find some of my other popular books that are popular on Amazon and Kindle as well. Alternatively, you can visit my author page on Amazon to see other work done by me.

How to Get Customers In Your Network Marketing Company

Network Marketing Mindset

Internet Marketing for Network Marketers

Network Marketing For Introverts

Bonus Video: How to Get Leads and Customers Online

Subscribe to Get Free Tips On How To Generate Leads and Get Customers

When you subscribe to get network marketing tips via email, you will get free access to exclusive subscriber-only resources. All you have to do is enter your email address to the right to get instant access.

These resources will help you get more out of your business – to be able to reach your goals, have more motivation, be at your best, and live the life you've always dreamed of. I'm always adding new resources, which you will be notified of as a subscriber. These will help you get an endless amount of leads and customers.

**Visit
www.networkmarketingkingdom.com/video
to Access The Bonus Video**